Other works by author:

My trilogy: Dragon Riders of The Realm, published by Xulon Press.

Book 1 - A Test of Faith and Friendship   2016 (Second Edition)

Book 2 - Caves of Conquest   2014

Book 3 - Uncharted Territory   2016

INTEGRITY AND GOD'S MAN

The Foundation and Formation of Integrity

JOHN W. TUCKER

WESTBOW PRESS®
A DIVISION OF THOMAS NELSON & ZONDERVAN

Scriptures taken from the Holy Bible, New International Version®, NIV®. Copyright © 1973, 1978, 1984, 2011 by Biblica, Inc.™ Used by permission of Zondervan. All rights reserved worldwide. www.zondervan.com The "NIV" and "New International Version" are trademarks registered in the United States Patent and Trademark Office by Biblica, Inc.™

This book is a work of non-fiction. Unless otherwise noted, the author and the publisher make no explicit guarantees as to the accuracy of the information contained in this book and in some cases, names of people and places have been altered to protect their privacy.

WestBow Press books may be ordered through booksellers or by contacting:

WestBow Press
A Division of Thomas Nelson & Zondervan
1663 Liberty Drive
Bloomington, IN 47403
www.westbowpress.com
1 (866) 928-1240

ISBN: 978-1-9736-4676-1 (sc)
ISBN: 978-1-9736-4675-4 (e)

Library of Congress Control Number: 2018914084

Print information available on the last page.

WestBow Press rev. date: 1/28/2019

CONTENTS

Four Biblical Character Studies

INTRODUCTION

Integrity touches all of life, including every thought, act, and word we speak. It comes to us from our Creator, for it reflects his character in us. Due to our fallen nature, we do not comprehend its full capacity to transform us into Christ's likeness, but this is God's will ultimately.

Integrity is God's plan for every Christian. It is the hub, center, and fulcrum of our lives in Christ. Integrity is Christ in us—the hope of glory. The apostle Paul pleaded with the Christians in the first century to let Christ be formed in them completely. True integrity is Christlikeness in its fullness in us.

What is integrity in our personal walk with Christ? How is it formed? What circumstances ensure its presence in us? What attitudes and lifestyle must we show for others to see Christ portrayed through us? This study is presented to open our hearts wider to God's plan for our understanding and growth in integrity.

Lessons 1–3c (five studies) give us an introduction to the scriptural definition of integrity. Lessons 4a and 4b establish the essential beliefs necessary for integrity (two lessons). Lessons 5–8 (six studies) describe the process, challenges, and potential consequences that will test our integrity. Lessons 9a–9d (four studies) give us a glimpse of our earthly and eternal rewards for faithful service (keeping integrity and holiness on the forefront of our lifestyle). Lessons 10a–10d (four character studies) help us see integrity in action through the eyes of true, biblical manhood. And lessons 11–12 (two studies) allow for a new definition of integrity and wrap up our time together.

Let's get started.

LESSON 1
What Does Integrity Look Like?

Years ago on a hot, sunny, spring morning, I pulled my wheelbarrow out of our garden shed in the backyard. It was buried under children's bicycles, rakes, and other interlocking items. Nevertheless, I retrieved it and set it on our cement patio for a good workout. My plan to haul dirt from our small garden to the rhubarb patch twenty feet away seemed doable. After filling the wheelbarrow three-fourths full, I grabbed the wooden handles and started my first run. As the front, rubber tire rolled its way over a garden hose and then over our bumpy lawn, I could feel the weight of the dirt tugging down on my hands and forearms. Stopping short of my destination, I set the load down and walked around the wheelbarrow, somewhat suspicious as to why it couldn't carry the dirt adequately.

"Aha!" I exclaimed. All the nuts and bolts were loose. Even the tire seemed full of air but lacked the strength to carry its present weight. I slowly moved the wheelbarrow to the rhubarb patch and parked it there. Examining the rhubarb, I noticed several weeds had cropped up and a few clumps of grass growing with the plants. After removing the weeds with a spade and transplanting the grass to needy areas in the yard, I dumped the dirt and spread it evenly among the rhubarb plants.

Then I returned to the patio and tipped the wheelbarrow upside down. Grabbing a few wrenches, screwdrivers, and my bike pump from the garage, I meticulously moved from bolt nut to bolt nut, tightening each one. After each tightening, I rechecked the previous one, ensuring its integrity to withstand the pressure and weight of future loads. I filled the front tire to its capacity. After turning the wheelbarrow over to its upright position, I grabbed the wooden handles, lifted them off the ground, and waddled the entire wheelbarrow back and forth, feeling its tightness and togetherness. It felt like one piece of equipment and not a bunch of loose nuts, bolts, and screws. What had I done?

First, I tested the integrity of the wheelbarrow by carrying a load of dirt across the yard. It did not meet the standards for what it was originally created to do. Second, I retightened the nut bolts and screws, making sure the handles and wedge assemblies were straight and properly positioned. Finally, I inflated the front tire to its capacity. These measures renewed the wheelbarrow's strength and nearly brought it back to its original condition. I restored its usefulness and prolonged its life simply by taking a few minutes to repair it.

Do you have integrity? Does it flow into every part of your life? Like the wheelbarrow, all the parts are there, but you have some loose screws. Let's begin with a few definitions.

Related Word Definitions

Character: *n.* 1. The combination of qualities or features that distinguishes one person, group, or thing from another. 2. A distinguishing feature or attribute, as of an individual, group, or category. 4. Moral or ethical strength. 7. Public estimation of someone; reputation.[1]

Character: *n.* 1. The aggregate of features and traits that form the individual nature of a person or thing. 2. One such feature or trait; characteristic. 3. Moral or ethical quality. 4. Qualities of honesty, fortitude, etc.; integrity.[2]

Core: *n.* 2. The central or innermost part. 3. The basic or most important part; the essence.[3]

Compromise: *n.* 1b. Something blending qualities of two different things. 2. To make a shameful or disreputable concession.[4]

Compromise: *tr.* 2. To expose or make liable to danger, suspicion, or disrepute. 3. A concession to something detrimental or pejorative: *a moral compromise.*[5]

Decay: *v.i.* 1. To become decomposed; rot. 2. To decline in health, prosperity, etc.; deteriorate. 6. A gradual and progressive decline. Syn. Decay, decompose, disintegrate, rot; imply a deterioration or falling away from a sound condition. Disintegrate emphasizes the breaking up, going to pieces, or wearing away of anything so that its original wholeness is impaired. *Rocks disintegrate.*[6]

Disintegrate: *v.* 1. To become reduced to components, fragments, or particles. 2. To lose cohesion or unity: *a family that disintegrated.*[7]

Foundation: *n.* 2. The basis on which a thing stands, is founded, or is supported.[8]

Foundation: *n.* 1. The basis or groundwork of anything: *the moral foundation of both society and religion.*[9]

Holiness: *n.* The moral quality of the character and actions of those who, through the indwelling of the Holy Spirit, share Christ's nature and consent to be ruled by it. C.f. Romans 6:22; 2 Corinthians 7:1; 1 Thessalonians 5:23; 1 John 1:7; 3:6–9.[10]

Integral: *adj.* 2. Possessing everything essential; entire.[11]

Integral: *adj.* 1. of or belonging as an essential part of the whole; necessary to completeness; constituent: *an integral part.* 2. Composed of parts that together constitute a whole. 3. Entire, complete, whole.[12]

Integrate: *v.* 1. To make a whole by bringing all parts together: unity. 2a. To join with something else; unity. 2b. To make part of a larger unit.[13]

Integrity: *n.* 1. Steadfast adherence to a strict ethical code. 2. The state of being unimpaired; soundness. 3. The quality or condition of being whole or undivided; completeness.[14]

Integrity: *n.* 1. Uncompromising adherence to moral and ethical principles; soundness of moral character; honesty. 2. The state of being whole or entire: *to preserve the integrity of the empire.* 3. A sound or unimpaired condition.[15]

Intricate: *adj.* 1. Having many complexly arranged elements; elaborate.[16]

Sanctity: *n.* 1. Holiness of life or disposition; saintliness. 2. The quality of condition of being considered sacred.[17]

Tenet: *n.* An opinion, doctrine, or principle held as truth by a person or esp. by an organization.[18]

My Definition

LESSON 2
How Integrity Is Used in Holy Scripture

1. Read Genesis 20:1–20, take notes, and discuss your position regarding Abraham's integrity and Abimelech's integrity.

2. Read and identify how integrity is used in each reference below:

Psalm 7:8

Psalm 25:21

Psalm 26:1, 11

Psalm 41:12

Psalm 101:2

Proverbs 2:7

Proverbs 10:9

Proverbs 19:1

Proverbs 20:7

Proverbs 28:6

LESSON 3A
How Integrity Is Implied in Holy Scripture

List the key words that imply the concept of integrity from these verses, and continue to think how you would define and explain the word *integrity:*

Deuteronomy 28:1–2

Psalm 15:1–5

Micah 6:8

LESSON 3B

More Implications

List the key words that imply the concept of integrity from these verses, and begin putting together a working definition of integrity:

1 Corinthians 13:4–8

Ephesians 6:10–20

LESSON 3C
More Implications

List key words that imply the concept of integrity from these verses, and add anything new to your working definition of *integrity*:

Titus 2:1–10

2 Peter 1:5–11

LESSON 4A
Foundations for a Life of Integrity

Try to come up with the missing words by reading the references. Meditate on these principles.

1. Without _____ and complete _____ in Jesus Christ, godly integrity cannot be obtained.

    • Psalm 4:5

    • Matthew 3:1–2

    • Acts 26:19–20

2. We must _____ and _____
   God's Holy Scriptures.

   - Genesis 22:15–18

   - 1 Timothy 4:13–16

   - Revelation 1:3

3. _____ in God (Father, Son, and Holy Spirit) is foundational to the Christian walk.

- Mark 11:22

- Galatians 3:11

- Hebrews 11:6

4. Growth in Christ comes through _____
   and produces_____ in the believer.

   - John 17:17

   - Ephesians 4:22–24

   - Colossians 2:6–7

   - Hebrews 5:11–14

5. God alone is _____ of everything. We are
   _____ under his authority.

   - Psalm 121:1–2

   - Luke 12:42–44

   - 1 Corinthians 4:1–2

LESSON 4B
More Foundations

Try to come up with the missing words by reading the references.

6. We must have the viewpoint that all human life, from conception, is_____.

   • Genesis 1:27

   • Psalm 139:15–16

   • Luke 12:23–24

7. We must recognize that God _____
   everyone and desires that we treat everyone with_____
   _____

   - Proverbs 3:12

   - John 3:16–17

   - James 2:1–4

8. We must not only _____ all others, but
   _____ them and do_____ to them.

   - Matthew 6:14–15

   - Luke 6:27–28, 35–36

   - Ephesians 4:32

9. Integrity (inner wholeness) and character (outer wholeness) develop over _____ and not without _____.

    •   Psalm 90:12

    •   Galatians 6:9–10

    •   Mark 1:35

    •   Philippians 4:6–7

10. Sincere _____ before God and others is basic to a life of integrity and personal _____ in Christ.

- Proverbs 11:2

- 1 Corinthians 3:6

- James 4:6

- 2 Peter 3:18

LESSON 5
The Growth of Integrity

Try to come up with the missing words by reading and writing down the meaning of the references.

A. _____ are part of life. We must learn from them. At times uncommon trials and unwanted _____ may also play a part in developing our integrity.

- Job 2:8–10

- John 15:20

- John 16:33

- 2 Timothy 2:3

- 1 Peter 1:6–9

B. Integrity cannot grow without _____.

- Psalm 133:1–3

- Acts 2:43–47

- 1 John 1:7

Someone once said, "We learn together to be one another." In other words, it is out of relationship that we begin to identify who we are, what our gifts are, and find direction toward our gifts or vocation.

C. Private time alone in God's presence to read, pray, _____, and, at times, _____, can lead to a life of integrity.

- Psalm 4:3–5, 7, 8

- Matthew 6:16–18

- Romans 15:4

- 2 Timothy 2:15

LESSON 6A
Hindrances to a Life of Integrity

Look up the passages and try to discover the word that goes in the blank. Briefly, write down the passage in your own words. List key points to the side.

1. Undetected _____, and its twin, self-promoting _____ hinder our walk with Christ.

    • Proverbs 8:13

    • Proverbs 11:2

    • Daniel 4:37

- Jude v. 16

2. Showing _____ for God in your thoughts, words, and actions will stop your movement toward integrity.

   - Deuteronomy 10:12, 13

   - 1 Samuel 12:24, 25

   - Luke 23:39–41

- 1 Corinthians 13:4–6

3. Forgetting that we will give an _____
   to God for how we lived on earth will make us look
   foolish in the eyes of our brothers and sisters in the
   Lord.

   - Joshua 7:10, 11, 20–26

   - 2 Corinthians 5:6–10

4. Ignoring the fact that we have a _____
    enemy will make us vulnerable to his attacks and derail
    our quest for a life of integrity.

    •   Job 1:9–11, 2:4, 5

    •   John 8:43, 44

    •   2 Corinthians 10:3–5

5. Taking our work, vocation, and _____
   lightly places us at odds with a life of integrity.

   - James 3:1, 2

   - 1 Timothy 4:15, 16

   - 2 Timothy 1:8–11

More Hindrances

6. Promoting the _____ of our eyes and our flesh lead to the death of our integrity.

- Proverbs 5:15–23

- Galatians 5:19–21

- 1 Thessalonians 4:3–8

- 1 John 2:16, 17

7. Practicing _____ sin while portraying a godly lifestyle leads to a false assurance regarding our Christian life and integrity.

- Psalm 44:20, 21

- Mark 4:22

- Romans 2:14–16

- 1 Corinthians 6:9–11

8. By _____ ourselves from one another and from the Body of Christ in fellowship and worship, we destroy our hope of leading a life of integrity.

- 1 Corinthians 12:14, 26

- Romans 15:30–33

- Hebrews 10:23–25

9. Lack of _____ and practicing
    _____ lead to destruction.

    - Proverbs 10:4, 5

    - Ecclesiastes 10:18

    - Matthew 25:26, 27

    - Hebrews 6:10–12

10. Accepting the _____ of others above that of Christ's will hinder our walk.

- Proverbs 27:21

- Matthew 6:2

- John 5:41–44

11. Withholding our _____ and
    _____ from the One who deserves
    it all weakens our example of integrity.

    • Psalm 89:5–8

    • Philippians 4:4–6

    • 1 Thessalonians 5:16–18

    • Revelations 4:9–11

LESSON 7A
Resisting the Misuse of Our Senses in Temptation

Read the passages and identify the human senses in each and how they were used.

- Proverbs 6:23–29

- Proverbs 7:6–27

LESSON 7B
Building Resilience to Temptation

Taking personal strides to improve our walk with Christ and remain accountable to other God-fearing men leads to a life of resilience to evil and all its subtle forms.

Read the passage prayerfully and identify characteristics of a godly man:

- Hebrews 5:12–6:3

- James 4:6–12

- Jude vv. 20–23

LESSON 8
Potential Consequences for Compromise

When we fall short of God's perfect will, His desire for us to be righteous before men, we may suffer consequences that try to keep us imprisoned. Over time we may hide our double lifestyle, or it seems that way, but eventually our sin will be discovered. Here are those potential outcomes of our waywardness and what we can do about them. There are five groups of consequences:

a. Group 1: shame, guilt, frustration, anger, unrest, self-loathing, perturbed, self-punishment, condemnation; hateful of cellphone, computer, television, free time, downtime, breaks away from work

b. Group 2: alienation, distance, bad pattern development, selfishness

c. Group 3: brokenness, mentally disturbed, anxiety, worry, misgivings about who I am, unforgiveness toward myself, pride in thinking I can make myself better, doubts about decisions I make, fear of God's disgust with me, regret

d. Group 4: complaining, blaming God and others, accusing, excusing, resentment, despondency

e. Group 5: divorce, jail time/prison, feeling lost/wandering, rejection by those we love, traffic tickets/citations, eviction, confusion, disease/infections, suicidal thoughts/suicide, etcetera.

Read these scriptures, write in your own words what they mean, and apply them to your heart. Know that God cares for you. Know that through faith in Jesus Christ, and through his blood sacrifice, all sin is forgiven.

- Hebrews 11:6

- 1 John 1:7–9

- 1 John 4:4

- 1 John 4:13–15

- 1 John 5:16–21

LESSON 9A
Standing in Integrity
Earthly Rewards

We're saved by grace, but we work out our salvation through fear and trembling (Philippians 2:12), honoring him through good deeds which he prepared in advance for us to do (Ephesians 2:10). Here are a few major highlights from Old and New Testaments that pinpoint the rewards that follow the life of the faithful. Look up the passages, list the earthly benefits, and ponder what great kindness our Lord offers us in rewards.

A. Earthly Rewards

1. Old Testament

   a. Deuteronomy 28:1–9

      Economic, political, and agricultural blessings … *find others.*

   b. Psalm 32: 5, 6, 10

      Salvation, instruction, forgiveness … *find others.*

c. Psalm 34:4–22

    Protection, provision, comfort, salvation …

d. Psalm 103:1–14

    Forgiveness, healing, honor, revelation …

e. Malachi 3:10–12

    Food, a name among the nations …

LESSON 9B
Standing in Integrity
More Earthly Rewards

2. New Testament

    a. Matthew 6:25–33

        Food, beverages, clothing …

    b. John 14:12–21

        Greater works, the Spirit of truth, revelation …

    c. Romans 5:1–5

        Peace, faith, character, hope, love …

d. Colossians 1:9–14

    Wisdom, understanding, power, patience …

e. 1 John 5:12–15

    Eternal life, confidence in prayer …

Standing in Integrity
Heavenly Rewards

A. Heavenly Rewards (of heaven or during the thousand-year reign)

   1. Old Testament

      a. Isaiah 61:1–10

         Freedom, restoration, joy, blessing …

      b. Joel 2:21–32

         Restoration, salvation …

      c. Zechariah 14:4–11

         Peace, security …

Standing in Integrity More Heavenly Rewards

2. New Testament

    a. Matthew 25:31–40

        Recognition, welcome …

    b. Ephesians 1:1–14

        Adoption, redemption, Holy Spirit …

c. Hebrews 11:13–16, 39, 40

    A better country …

d. Revelation 2:7, 11, 17, 23b, 26–28; 3:5, 9–12, 21

    Eating, protection, a name, gifts, authority …

FOUR BIBLICAL CHARACTER STUDIES

Abraham's Servant (Genesis 24)

1. What were his specific responsibilities?

2. How did he handle the specific problems he encountered?

3. What character traits show up in his handling of responsibility?

4. How thorough was his account at the end of his journey?

5. What do you identify with regarding his responsibility to Abraham, and what do you see lacking in your own life in this regard?

Boaz (Ruth 2-4)

1. How does Boaz conduct himself as an employer?

2. How does Boaz conduct himself in personal relationships?

3. How does Boaz show himself a champion of righteousness in the way he seeks to redeem Ruth?

4. What rewards come to Boaz for his treatment of Ruth?

5. How does the way Boaz treated others compare to the way you treat them? (Employer to employee, citizen to stranger, kinsman redeemer to distant relative, friend to friend, husband to wife)

LESSON 10C

Jesus (John 4:34, 5:30, 8:29, 12:26, 13:14, 14:15, 16:24, 18:37, 20:29, 21:19; Hebrews 5:7–9)

1. Whom does Jesus follow obediently? How does our Lord's subordination relate to integrity in the Christian walk?

2. In what ways does obedience lead to maturity and the development of integrity?

3. Name some commands/words of Christ that we are to obey.

4. Jesus was a man of the highest integrity. Name four character traits he had that you want to develop or are presently developing in your own walk of faith.

5. Do you ever cry out to God, shed tears, or sob? Jesus did these on different occasions: in prayer, at funerals, because of people's waywardness, or when life's troubles came his way. If it's hard for you to cry, please share why. Does our integrity depend on how spontaneous our emotions are? Why or why not?

LESSON 10D
Saul/Paul the Apostle (Acts 8:1–3; Philippians 3:4–9; Acts 9:1–9, 17–20; 1 Timothy 3:1–10, 12, 13)

1. What was Saul like before his conversion? Can you relate to Saul's attitude toward Christians before you were converted? How and where were you converted to Christ?

2. After Paul's conversion, he changed his message and attitude toward the followers of Jesus. How does integrity change our message and attitude toward one another as professing Christians?

3. In what ways did Paul look at his credentials and exchange their glory for the glory of God? In what ways do you exchange your titles, credentials, and past experiences for the greater reward of bringing Christ glory?

4. Pastors and leaders in the church are required to live lives of integrity. Share your thoughts about Paul's list of qualifications for pastors and leaders. Are they realistic, doable, and on your list to pursue?

LESSON 11
My New Definition of Integrity

1. Write it out here:

2. What is similar to my first definition?

3. What is different from my first definition?

4. What changed and why?

LESSON 12
Wrap Up

Final Thoughts

1. What scripture portions affected you the most in your study on integrity?
    List them and be ready to share one or two.

2. Has anything changed in your view of integrity? If so, what?

3. How do you hope to apply what you've learned from this study?

Tips for Leading Group Discussions

➢ Know the approximate amount of time the group has for discussion.

➢ Try to give everyone an opportunity to speak to the questions, verses.

➢ Encourage everyone to write down their answers to the scripture verses listed for each study and come prepared to share.

➢ Do one or two lessons a week if time permits.

➢ Always try to end discussions on a positive note.

➢ Feel free to integrate the following questions/illustrations throughout this Bible study time. Challenge students/members to think in practical terms and real-life examples of how, where, when, their integrity is evident in everyday circumstances.

➢ Feel free to come up with your own Q/A sessions to keep the discussions relevant.

Five Illustrations for Evaluating My Integrity

1. Place two musical instruments of the same kind, one in need of repair and the other brand-new or in great condition, next to each other. Let the group discuss which one has more integrity and why.

2. Ask the group to discuss the building project of a house and what would be required for that house to be built with integrity.

3. Place three or more pieces of wood before the group (pine, oak, maple, cherry, cedar, or so on). Ask for discussion on the integrity of each piece: soft versus hard, strong versus weak, usefulness in furniture or other projects, beauty when sanded and stained, durability over time, and other characteristics. Compare the pieces to different personalities they have known. Discuss integrity in light of these aspects.

4. Place a Bible and another famous book next to each other in the center of the group. Discuss the integrity of each book and how the structure, interpretation, and challenges of each book apply to the integrity in their own lives.

5. Discuss the integrity of the building you are meeting in. Was it once in better shape than it is today? Could it be improved with a bit of upkeep and handiwork? Relate the

discussion to your own lives. What will it take to improve or maintain your own level of integrity?

Potential Environments That Will Test My Integrity
(How will I think, speak, and act?)

A. Home Life

1. How do I control my temper in a family setting, with kids present?

2. Have I planned ahead to discuss family matters in a polite and engaging manner in the privacy of a parental meeting?

3. What do I do to control my thoughts and actions when home alone with no one around?

4. Am I pleasant to work with when doing household chores with others? What makes for a great work time together?

B. On the Job

1. How are my attendance record, appearance, and attitude at work? (If you are without a job, are you pleasant to live with while seeking a job?)

2. Am I respecting company employees and property? How does my work ethic show I care?

3. In what ways am I accurate and honest in my paperwork and conversations?

4. Is confidentiality kept with all information as required?

5. How do I share my faith without offending others?

C. At the Grocery Store, Gas Station, or Department Store

1. Do I respect property, product, and personnel? Am I polite in my manners?

2. Do I listen actively and give focused attention to those I am with and to others with whom I engage in conversation?

3. Do I leave the place as good or better than I found it?

D. Public Meetings and Sporting Events

1. Respecting others around me by sharing the seats and welcoming strangers into my area can say a lot about my lifestyle. Is this expected of me? Why or why not?

2. Do I control my attitude and temper when things don't go my way? Give an example.

3. Do I cheer for my team without demeaning the other team in some way? Even silence can be a witness. Am I willing to share my comments calmly and briefly as needed?

4. Do I value relationships more than who wins the game or whose side wins in a debate? Give an example.

5. When exiting large events, am I willing to let others ahead of me so order can be maintained? Are my manners evident in various challenges? In what ways can I be a servant?

More Potential Environments

E. Traffic Jams, Accidents, Traveling

1. In traffic, do I leave early enough to arrive safely and in good spirits to my destination, with time to spare? If I'm running late, do I make excuses, apologize, or speak the truth in practical terms?

2. How can I show politeness when exchanging information between drivers in lieu of an accident (when I am involved with my vehicle)?

3. How do I prepare and work with my family when on vacation to ensure everyone has a good time?

4. In what ways do I stay clear of reckless drivers and not let others control my driving and attitude?

F. Tragedies/Death in the Family

1. Do I ask for time off from work to attend the funeral of a relative, even if we weren't that close?

2. Being able to express my grief in a loss and share stories of the good times we had together if the opportunity comes to do so: Is this a good goal? Keeping the negative stuff to myself, showing respect for the deceased, would be the best plan. Do you agree? Why or why not?

3. Do I allow the grief process to work through my soul, taking time to consider the shortness of life on this earth?

G. In Trouble with the Law

1. Obeying the laws of the land as best as is God's way to maneuver in traffic. Do you agree?

2. When pulled over for speeding or other traffic violations, courtesy and cooperation with peace officers is our responsibility. Explain how that can be done.

3. When arrested for serious violations or caught for criminal activities, do I repent and change my ways to honor Christ, or do I resist and seek more harm than good?

4. When running from the law, do I quickly realize my mistake and turn myself in, giving the Lord opportunity to change my heart, with his help?

H. On My Own Deathbed

1. How do you plan to look back on times that you and the Lord have done well together?

2. Think of your past friendships, mentors, teachers, and relatives that have helped you come to this point in your life. Share a highlight of one that meant a lot to you.

3. In what way could my last words be helpful and encouraging to those by my bedside or wherever I am at my last breath?

4. Did I take time to prepare a will so my family can bury/cremate me peacefully? If not, why not do it now?

5. Other circumstances not listed here that will test my integrity.

Quotations to Ponder

Read and consider the impact of each statement, quotation. or saying. Discuss each one and share your thoughts.

1. "Character is not made in crisis—it is only exhibited." (Freeman) [17]
2. "Sow a thought, reap an act; sow an act, reap a habit; sow a habit, reap a character; sow a character, reap a destiny." [18]
3. "Character is simply long habit continued." (Plutarch) [19]
4. "Only what we have wrought into our character during life can we take with us." (Humboldt) [20]
5. "His goal is not to pamper us physically but to perfect us spiritually." (Paul W. Powel) [21]

[All quotations were taken from Charles R. Swindoll, *The Quest For Character*, Multnomah Press, Portland, Oregon, 1987]

(Please feel free to write or email the author your comments, questions, suggestions at: cstm. jtucker@gmail.com. Thank you.)

APPENDIX
Definitions from Others

"A prominent businessman once replied to a question: 'If I had to name the one most important quality of a top manager, I would say, *personal integrity*.' **Surely the spiritual leader must be sincere in promise, faithful in discharge of duty, upright in finances, loyal in service, and honest in speech.**

"When people try to take the measure of [James] Dobson, they often list his talents and attributes, concluding that he possesses a rare combination. For example, 'he's a remarkable combination of entrepreneur, biblical thinker, detailed administrator, stunningly effective communicator, and visionary,' says Charlie Jarvis, once a senior staffer at Focus and later Gary Bauer's presidential campaign manager. 'Those almost never all exist in a single person. That almost always has to be a combination of people. He is all of those things and at the same time he's personable.'" [1]

During a chapel service at the Dallas Theological Seminary in 2011, Charles Swindoll shared his own insights on integrity. **"A person with integrity, 'is verbally responsible, financially accountable, personally reliable, privately pure, ethically sound, will not commit plagiarism, and has moral excellence."** He went on to share six benefits of a person of integrity: **"They will have 1. Sustained cultivation of exemplary character; 2. Continued relief of a clear conscience; 3. The personal delight of intimacy with God; 4. The priceless inheritance of an unsoiled legacy; 5. The rare privilege of being a mentor; and 6. The crowning reward of finishing well."** I found his message about integrity on video from a Google website. [2]

Look at integrity as a verb, noun, or adjective. It has powerful implications for our walk of faith. These definitions may bring conviction on our hearts because we all fall short of God's ideal for us as men. The truth is, if we haven't made Christ the center of our lives, integrity and godlike character do not have a chance to grow in us.

How does God define integrity?

"**Integrity**: The state or quality of being complete, well adjusted. It implies sincerity of heart and motive, singleness of purpose, genuineness, truthfulness, uprightness. In Biblical thought moral character is not judged by any absolute or ideal (as in Greek philosophy), but by relationship to God. God sets the standard by which man is judged. That man alone is perfect who is so in the judgment of God. Integrity thus marks the man who walks with single-hearted devotion to God and honorable behavior to men (Proverbs 25:21). The whole drama of redemption is centered on the possibility of the sinner walking in uprightness before God." [3]

NOTES

Lesson 1

1   (Character) *The American Heritage College Dictionary*. New York: Houghton Mifflin Company, 2004. p. 242.

2   (Character) *Random House Webster's Collegiate Dictionary*. New York: Random House, 1997. p. 220.

3   (Core) Ibid., *American Heritage*, p. 317.

4   (Compromise) *Webster's New Collegiate Dictionary*. Springfield: G. & C. Merriam Company, 1975. p. 232.

5   (Compromise) Ibid., *American Heritage*, p. 295.

6   (Decay) Ibid., *Random House*, p. 341.

7   (Disintegrate) Ibid., *American Heritage*, p. 406.

8   (Foundation) Ibid., *American Heritage*, p. 547.

9   (Foundation) Ibid., *Random House*, p. 513.

10 (Holiness) Harrison, Everett F. *Baker's Dictionary of Theology*. Grand Rapids: Baker Book House, 1960. p. 269–270.

11 (Integral) Ibid., *American Heritage*, p. 720.

12 (Integral) Ibid., *Random House*, p. 678.

13 (Integrate) Ibid., *American Heritage*, p. 720.

14 (Integrity) Ibid., *American Heritage,* p. 721.

15 (Integrity) Ibid., *Random House*, p. 678.

16 (Intricate) Ibid., *American Heritage,* p. 727–728.

17 (Sanctity) Ibid., *American Heritage,* p. 1228.

18 (Tenet) Ibid., *American Heritage,* p. 1420.

Appendix

1   Buss, Dale. *Family Man: The Biography of Dr. James Dobson*. Wheaton: Tyndale House Publishers, 2005. p. 198–199.

2   Swindoll, Charles. Chapel Service Message, Dallas Theological Seminary, 2011.

3   *The Interpreter's Dictionary of the Bible*. Nashville: Abingdon Press, 1962. p. 718.

Printed in the United States
By Bookmasters